SAVING WILDLIFE

Wetland Animals

Sonya Newland

W
FRANKLIN WATTS
LONDON • SYDNEY

First published in 2011 by
Franklin Watts
338 Euston Road
London NW1 3BH

Franklin Watts Australia
Level 17/207 Kent Street
Sydney NSW 2000

Produced for Franklin Watts by
White-Thomson Publishing
+44 (0)843 208 7460
www.wtpub.co.uk

Series consultant: Sally Morgan
Designer: Clare Nicholas
Picture researcher: Amy Sparks

A CIP catalogue record for this book is available from the British Library.

ISBN: 978 0 7496 9546 0

Dewey Classification: 591.7'68

Picture Credits
Dreamstime: Cover (Barbara Helgason), 8 (Stef Bennett), 23b (Paul Edwards); **NHPA:** 25b (Ken Griffiths); **Nature Picture Library:** 9t (Ingo Arndt), 10 (Rod Williams); **Photolibrary:** 5 (Colin Milkins), 7 (Shoot Shoot), 13t (Nigel Pavitt), 15t (Fritz Polking), 17t (Nature Picture Library), 18 (Andrew McLachlan), 19t (David M. Dennis), 19b (Emanuele Biggi), 20 (Austin J. Stevens), 21b (Bert and Babs Wells), 24b (Oxford Scientific), 26t (AIC), 26b (Juniors Bildarchiv); **Shutterstock:** 4 (iofoto), 6 (FloridaStock), 9b (Graeme Shannon), 11t (siloto), 11b (Rudy Umans), 12 (Eduardo Rivero), 13b (Daniel Rajszczak), 14 (Tony Campbell), 15b (H.Damke), 16 (Martha Marks), 21t (mlorenz), 22 (Pressurepics), 23t (P. Schwarz), 24t (Vasiliy Koval), 25t (Cheryl Casey), 27 (mlorenz); **United States Fish & Wildlife Service:** 17b (Adam Mann).

Every attempt has been made to clear copyright. Should there be any inadvertent omission, please apply to the publisher for rectification.

Printed in China

Franklin Watts is a division of Hachette Children's Books, an Hachette UK Company.
www.hachette.co.uk

Contents

Words in **bold** are in the glossary on page 31.

Wetland Habitats

Wetlands are some of the world's most important environments. Because they are made up of both land and water, they are home to thousands of types of plants and animals.

What is a wetland?

Wetlands are areas where the ground is covered with water for some of the year. Although the water does not usually flow in or out, the amount of water in a wetland region depends on the season. In hot summer months the pools of standing water can dry up, while in the rainy season almost all the land might be covered. All sorts of creatures live in wetlands – from tiny midges to huge crocodiles.

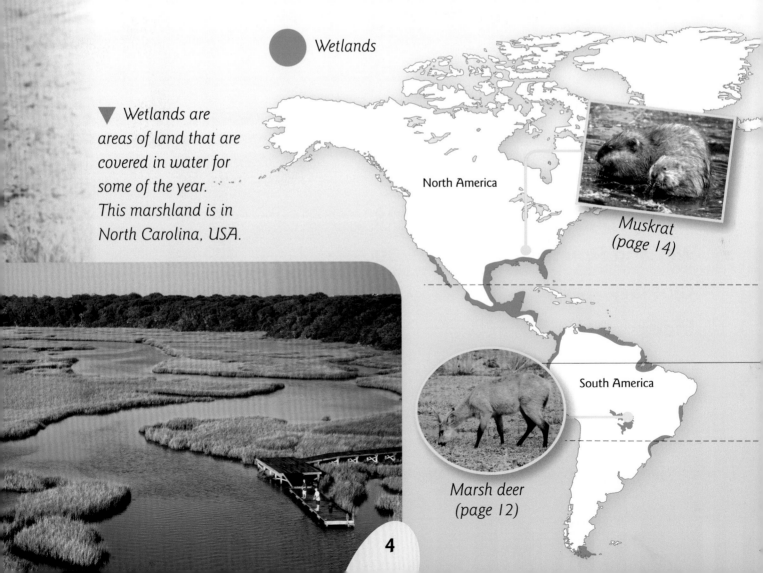

● Wetlands

▼ *Wetlands are areas of land that are covered in water for some of the year. This marshland is in North Carolina, USA.*

North America

Muskrat
(page 14)

South America

Marsh deer
(page 12)

Types of wetland

The main types of wetland are swamps, marshes, bogs and floodplains. Each one is home to different plants and animals. Swamps can be made up of **freshwater** or **saltwater**, and they often have tall trees growing in them. Marshes are similar to swamps, but they have more grasses than trees. Bogs have a spongy soil called **peat**. The plants that grow there are usually mosses or reeds. Floodplains are areas around rivers that flood when the river overflows. Other types of wetland include **fens**, ponds and **mangroves**.

▼ *This map shows the world's largest wetland areas, although wetlands can be found in almost every country.*

EXTREME ANIMALS

Wetland water scorpions have been nicknamed 'toe-biters' because of their painful nip. They can seize fish larger than themselves with their sharp pincers.

2 cm

Gharial (page 11)

Europe

Asia

Africa

Tropic of Cancer

Equator

Western swamp tortoise (page 21)

Tropic of Capricorn

Australia

Hippo (page 9)

Wetlands Under Threat

Over the last 100 years, more than half of all the wetlands in the world have disappeared, as humans have taken the land and water to meet their own needs.

Where have the wetlands gone?

For years, people regarded wetlands as wastelands that could be turned into useful land for farming or to live on. **Pollution** from farming and factories has poisoned the water. Wetland water has been channelled away for **irrigation**. **Climate change** is also affecting wetlands, as hotter summers mean there is less water.

Birds such as this heron in Florida, USA, need wetlands to wade in to catch fish.

Why are wetlands important?

Wetlands stop flooding by taking in water like a sponge. They also help to purify water (see page 18). When water levels are low, wetlands slowly release water and plant matter into rivers and surrounding areas, keeping other **habitats** healthy. They are vital for thousands of **species** that live there all year round, or use them as stopovers during **migration** or for **breeding**.

ENDANGERED ANIMALS

The International Union for Conservation of Nature (IUCN, see page 28) lists animals according to how **endangered** they are.

Extinct: Died out completely.

Extinct in the wild: Only survive in captivity – for example, in zoos.

Critically endangered: Extremely high risk of becoming extinct in the near future.

Endangered: High risk of becoming extinct in the wild.

Vulnerable: High risk of becoming endangered in the wild.

Near threatened: Likely to become endangered in the near future.

Least concern: Lowest risk of becoming endangered.

Saving the world's wetlands

As wetlands have dried up or become polluted, many of the animals that live there have become endangered. Fish and other aquatic creatures die out, and there is not enough food and water for animals further up the **food chain**. People now realise how important wetlands are. In 1975, an agreement known as Ramsar was set up between the governments of many different countries, to help restore and manage wetland areas all over the world.

▲ *Fish die because of pollution in wetland waters. This also affects the animals that feed on them.*

7

Large Mammals

Most big animals need large areas of land to hunt and breed in, so few are found in the world's wetlands. However, some large creatures make their homes around swamps and floodplains.

Cats of the Pantanal

The Pantanal in Brazil, South America, is the largest wetland area in the world. Among the most powerful **predators** there are jaguars. Worldwide, jaguars are near threatened through habitat loss and killing by farmers protecting their **livestock**. Hunting is now banned in many South American countries. In the Pantanal, 'jaguar safaris' – where people are taken on tours to see the big cats – have become a tourist attraction. The money this brings in is used to help **conservation** efforts.

▼ *Jaguars enjoy swimming, so they are at home in the watery habitat of the South American Pantanal.*

Endangered elephants live in the swamp forests of Asian countries such as India and Sumatra.

Asian elephants

There are no more than 32,750 Asian elephants left in the wild, as people cut down their swamp forest habitat and hunt them for their **tusks**. Through the Asian Rhino and Elephant Action Strategy (AREAS), the WWF (see page 28) has set up national parks and **reserves** in areas where they live. This protects them from hunting and the effects of **logging**.

Apes of the swamp forests

Lowland gorillas of African swamp forests were thought to be nearly extinct. However, recently a **census** revealed that around 125,000 gorillas were living in the swamp forests of the Republic of Congo. Although this is twice the number previously thought to be found worldwide, they are still critically endangered, and the WWF, the Wildlife Conservation Society (WCS) and other groups work to protect them.

▶ *This hippo has swamp plants on its back from wading in the muddy water.*

SAVING WILDLIFE

Hippopotamus

Habitat loss, **drought** and **civil war** have all put Africa's swamp-dwelling hippos under threat. There are estimated to be 125,000–148,000 left in the wild, up to one-fifth fewer than there were just 10 years ago. Although the IUCN has conservation programmes to study and preserve hippo populations, numbers are still decreasing in many countries. However, they are stable and even increasing in countries including Zambia, Chad and Ethiopia.

Crocs in the Swamps

Crocodiles, alligators, caimans and gharials belong to a group of animals called crocodilians. These fearsome creatures are most at home in swamps, rivers and lakes in warmer parts of the world.

Threatened crocodilians

Several of the 23 species of crocodilians are endangered. In some places their wetland homes have been lost as humans have settled on the land. Hunting has also threatened crocodiles, because their skin is used to make expensive shoes and bags, and crocodile meat is a popular food in some countries.

Philippine crocodiles

The Philippine crocodile is critically endangered – there are only 100 of them left in their natural habitat. Some of the animals have been bred in captivity, and in 2009 an IUCN-sponsored programme released 50 of them into the wild. This programme may prevent the species dying out altogether.

▲ *Philippine crocodiles are threatened by habitat loss, as people drain the crocs' wetland homes so they can live there.*

WHAT DO YOU THINK?

Around 2,000 people a year are attacked by crocodiles and alligators. Do you think it is acceptable for humans to kill animals out of fear, or should all endangered creatures have the same level of protection?

Indian gharials

There are fewer than 200 Indian gharials left in the wild. The Gharial Conservation Alliance has released around 5,000 **captive bred** gharials into the wild over the past 30 years, but the programme has not been successful. Many of the crocs died from an unknown disease that may have been caused by water pollution.

▲ *Indian gharials can be identified by their very long, narrow snout.*

SAVING WILDLIFE

American alligator

By the 1960s, numbers of American alligators had dropped so much through habitat loss and hunting that it was feared they could not be saved. However, the US Fish and Wildlife Service set up large alligator farms, and hunting was made illegal. These steps helped the population recover, and there are now more than a million alligators in the wild.

▶ *Thanks to conservation efforts, American alligators are now listed as of least concern by the IUCN.*

Deer and Antelope

Many deer and antelope live around wetland areas, where they feed on aquatic plants. Some are particularly well suited to these watery landscapes.

Marsh deer

Marsh deer of the South American Pantanal are listed as vulnerable by the IUCN. In the past they were hunted by humans for their antlers, but now hunting is strictly controlled. However, marsh deer are facing new threats, including diseases caught from cattle and habitat loss as parts of the Pantanal are turned into land for farming and livestock grazing.

▼ *Marsh deer feed on the plants that grow in the South American Pantanal.*

EXTREME ANIMALS

Marsh deer are the largest deer species in South America, reaching 2 m in length.

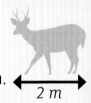

2 m

African antelope

Lechwe antelope of southern Africa feed on water plants, so they are usually found in marshland and floodplains. Although they are considered low risk, they are also 'conservation dependent'. This means that if their habitat is not protected, the antelope may become more endangered. The building of **hydroelectric dams** to create electricity from the flowing water in their habitat is one of the biggest threats to the lechwe.

▶ *Lechwe antelope have a special water-repellant substance on their legs, which allows them to move quickly across the floodplains.*

Sitatunga

The sitatunga is an aquatic antelope that lives in swamps in Africa. Although these unusual animals are only considered near threatened, little is known about them and experts are worried that hunting and habitat destruction may pose problems in the future. In an effort to find out more about them, some sitatunga have been moved to the Lewa Wildlife Conservancy, a **sanctuary** in Kenya, where they can be protected and studied.

▼ *Female sitatungas, such as this one, have reddish-brown fur, while males are greyish-brown.*

Semi-aquatic Creatures

'Semi-aquatic' animals live on land, but spend a lot of time in the water. In particular, several large semi-aquatic rodents live in wetland habitats, including muskrats, beavers and capybara.

Marsh-loving muskrats

Muskrats make their homes in swamps, marshes, lakes and ponds. Hunting for their fur once meant they were threatened in the wild, but these hardy **mammals** survived. They bred quickly and **adapted** well to different habitats, so populations are now stable. In some places, muskrats are even considered **pests**, and are deliberately trapped to keep their numbers down.

▼ *Muskrats were once widely hunted for their fur, but now they are plentiful across wetlands in North America.*

▼ *A giant otter feeds on a fish in the Brazilian Pantanal, South America.*

1.6 m

SAVING WILDLIFE

Giant otter

By the 1980s, there were fewer than 3,000 giant otters left in the wetlands of South America because so many had been hunted for their velvety fur. Captive breeding by groups including the International Otter Survival Fund helped numbers to rise, and for a while it seemed that the giant otter had been saved. Today, the IUCN estimates the number of giant otters is dropping again. This is because of water pollution, caused especially by the **mercury** used in gold mining, which poisons the fish eaten by the otters.

Capybaras and coypus

Capybaras and coypus are rodents that live in the swamps, marshes, rivers and lakes of South America. Throughout the nineteenth century, they were widely hunted for their meat and fur, and numbers dropped dramatically. However, when hunting of these creatures began to be controlled, and farms were set up for captive breeding, populations rose again. Coypus have also been introduced to North America and Europe, where they thrive in the wild.

EXTREME ANIMALS

Capybaras are the largest rodents in the world, growing up to 1.3 m long.

Small Mammals

Small mammals such as rabbits, mice, shrews and squirrels are important to the wetland habitat. They are a key part of the food chain, as they are preyed on by larger mammals and birds of prey.

Rabbits of swamps and marshes

Marsh rabbits inhabit marshland in coastal areas of the USA, while larger swamp rabbits are more often found in inland wetland areas. Unlike most other types of rabbit, marsh and swamp rabbits are strong swimmers, and never travel too far from water. The reeds and other water plants that they feed on are essential for their survival, so unless their wetland homes are protected from human activity, these unusual rabbits may come under threat.

▼ *Although not yet listed as endangered, swamp rabbits are considered 'vulnerable' in states such as Kentucky and Arkansas.*

Little rodents

Water voles and water shrews are two of the smaller members of the rodent family. They once thrived in wetland areas, but are now becoming increasingly threatened. They have been given **protected status** in some countries, including the UK, where they are being killed by American mink, an **introduced species**. Several conservation organisations are helping these little rodents by controlling mink populations and breeding voles in captivity.

90 mm

▶ *Water shrews, such as this one in the UK, have water-repellent fur that keeps them dry and warm in the damp environment.*

EXTREME ANIMALS

Water shrews are believed to have poisonous spit that can cause a human burning pain for days.

SAVING WILDLIFE

Grey bat

The endangered grey bat of the southern USA lives in caves near wetland areas and feeds on aquatic insects. The US Fish and Wildlife Service has started a recovery plan that includes stopping tourists from disturbing the bats, which is one of the main threats to their survival. Other conservation organisations work towards protecting their habitat – both the caves in which they live and the wetlands that they need to survive.

▲ *Grey bats sleep during the day and search for their insect prey at night.*

Amphibians

Wetlands are important for amphibians such as frogs, toads and salamanders. They live partly on land, but need water to lay their eggs, so wetlands are the perfect home.

Frogs and toads

Numbers of many species of frogs and toads have dropped over the past 50 years, and this may be because wetlands are disappearing. When swamps are drained, there is nowhere for the animals to breed and feed. Organisations such as the Wildfowl and Wetlands Trust are working all over the world to monitor and research amphibian populations, and to create and restore wetland habitats.

▲ *Vernal pools are especially important breeding grounds for* **amphibians** *such as American toads, because there are no fish to eat the eggs before they can hatch.*

WHAT DO YOU THINK?

Wetlands can purify water, cleaning out pollutants from industry and agriculture. This natural process is a benefit to people, but it can change the wetland environment. Is it right to create artificial wetlands as part of the purification process, even if it harms the animals that will make their home there?

Slimy salamanders

Although some salamanders live on land, others – such as the mudpuppy – never lose the **gills** that they are born with, and stay underwater their whole lives. Several species, including blue-spotted and tiger salamanders, have become endangered through water pollution or because their wetland pools have dried up.

▶ A four-toed salamander in the USA buries its eggs in the damp earth near the water.

▲ Hellbenders usually feed on fish or insects, but they will also prey on small mammals such as this mouse.

Hellbender
The giant North American salamander called the hellbender has come under threat since the 1970s. The water has become more polluted and dams have changed the natural flow of water in their wetland homes. Different states in the USA have their own conservation programmes, mostly aimed at restoring wetlands as a whole. These groups hope that by protecting their habitat, numbers of hellbenders will rise again naturally.

Reptiles

Reptiles do not depend on wetlands as much as amphibians do. Swamps, marshes, bogs and fens are still important reptile habitats, though, because while they lay their eggs on land, many young reptiles spend their early lives in the water.

Swamp snakes

Swamps are home to several snakes, including northern watersnakes, mud snakes and poisonous water moccasins. Even some tree snakes can be found in wetland woodlands. The enormous endangered anaconda lurks in swamps in South America, moving swiftly through the water to catch its prey of fish or water mammals.

EXTREME ANIMALS

The green anaconda is the heaviest snake in the world – the heaviest ever recorded was 97 kg.

5 m

▲ *Many species of turtles rely on wetlands for survival.*

Threatened turtles

Wetlands are particularly important habitats for turtles because they are more aquatic than other reptiles. This means they are more affected by changes to the wetland environment caused by drainage, human disturbance or pollution. Species such as pig-nosed, snake-necked and bog turtles are already endangered, but governments and national conservation groups are cleaning up wetland areas and protecting this habitat to save them from dying out.

SAVING WILDLIFE

Western swamp tortoise

Western swamp tortoises are the most endangered **reptile** in Australia. By the 1980s there were only around 30 left in the wild, in coastal areas of Perth, Western Australia. The WWF has worked with the Australian government on programmes to save these tortoises, including restoring swamps and captive breeding. Numbers of the tortoises are now slowly rising.

▶ *Western swamp tortoise.*

1.5 cm

Wetland Birds

The abundance of insects and other small creatures in wetlands attracts thousands of bird species to these areas. They also use them for breeding, nesting and raising their young.

Permanent settlers

Some water birds, such as herons and flamingos, live in wetlands all year round. They stay in the shallows, feeding on aquatic plants and snapping up fish. Although some water birds have adapted to other habitats as wetlands dry up or become polluted, other species rely on wetlands so much that they cannot survive without them. Wetland destruction and **degradation** have a big impact on these birds.

▼ *Numbers of flamingos in Africa are dropping, possibly because pesticides are polluting wetland areas.*

22

Wetland visitors

Other birds only use wetlands for part of the year or for part of their lives, such as when they are breeding. Wetlands are important stopovers for migrating birds, such as plovers and sandpipers, providing places where they can rest and find food. Birds of prey such as fish eagles and osprey also live around coastal plains, rivers and marshes, feeding on the fish and small mammals that live there.

Birds such as ospreys rely on wetlands to provide them with fish for food.

Oil exploration in Russia, where red-breasted geese spend the summer, has contributed to their population decline.

Minibeasts

▲ *Water skaters seem to 'skate' on the top of the water, using their water-repelling legs.*

Insects and bugs thrive in wetland areas. Some live near or on the water, but others make their homes beneath the surface – even in the muddy depths. They are essential to the wetland environment.

Amazing adaptations

Insects have adapted to wetland environments in many different ways. Those that live under the water may store air so they can breathe. Others, such as water boatmen and water scorpions, suck in air through a hollow spine on their bodies. Some insects, such as water skaters and mosquitoes, live on the surface of the water.

EXTREME ANIMALS

Whirligig beetles' eyes are divided in two so they can see above and below the surface of the water at the same time.

6 mm

Butterfly paradise

Butterflies flourish in wetlands because of the thousands of different plants there. Some butterfly species, including the swamp metalmark and Mitchell's satyr butterfly, both found in the USA, are now endangered, as their habitat has been cleared for human settlement. Recovery plans are in place for these insects. They include captive breeding, and re-establishing swamps and bogs.

▶ *Butterflies play an important role in the wetland* **ecosystem** *by* **pollinating** *the flowers.*

▲ *The giant dragonfly is one of the world's largest, and is found only along the east coast of Australia.*

SAVING WILDLIFE

Giant dragonfly

Threatened by habitat clearance, disturbance and water pollution, Australia's giant dragonfly was listed as endangered in the 1980s. The country's Department of Environment and Conservation has begun a series of programmes designed to stop them dying out. These include protecting their swamp home from pollution and reintroducing natural water flow to the habitats. It will be some years before the success of these programmes is known, though.

Fish and Shellfish

Inland wetlands that change with the seasons are not ideal places for fish to live permanently, but coastal wetlands are particularly important habitats for fish and shellfish.

▲ *Sea trout, which breed in coastal wetlands, feed on insects and smaller fish.*

Breeding zones

Fish that normally live out in the oceans, such as bass and sea trout, often come to **estuaries** for breeding and raising their young, before heading out to the open water again. Shellfish such as oysters and clams also use coastal wetlands for food and shelter. These species are commercially important, because they are caught to sell for food. When coastal wetlands are destroyed, the numbers of these fish drop and commercial fishing is affected.

EXTREME ANIMALS

Mudskipper fish can survive out of water for up to two days at a time, using their fins as legs.

15 cm

The wetland food chain

Along with insects, fish, shellfish and **crustaceans** play a critical role in the wetland ecosystem as part of the food chain. All of them are a food source for the larger animals and birds that live there. As water is drained away and wetland areas shrink, fewer fish can live there and this has an effect on other wetland wildlife. If the water becomes polluted, it is not just the fish that are affected. The poisons they swallow can kill the creatures that eat them. Keeping wetlands free of pollution is key to the survival of all the creatures in this habitat.

▶ *An anhinga eats a fish in the USA. These diving birds feast on fish and amphibians in the wetland environment.*

WHAT DO YOU THINK?

Many fish species are dying out because too many of them have been caught to feed the growing human population. Which is more important – feeding people or saving wildlife?

What Can We Do?

Wetlands are some of the most important habitats in the world for both humans and animals. People have now realised how important it is to manage wetlands properly, and to conserve the plants and animals that live there. Local, national and international organisations work hard to do this, but there are ways that everyone can help.

Find out more...

WWF *(www.wwf.org.uk)*

This is the UK site of the largest international animal conservation organisation. On this site you can follow links to information on all sorts of endangered animals, and find out what the WWF is doing to save wetland creatures.

EDGE of Existence *(www.edgeofexistence.org)*

The EDGE of Existence is a special global conservation programme that focuses on saving what it calls evolutionarily distinct and globally endangered (EDGE) species – unusual animals and plants that are under threat.

International Union for Conservation of Nature *(www.iucn.org)*

The IUCN produces the Red List, which lists all the world's known endangered species and classifies them by how under threat they are, from least concern to extinct. You can see the whole list of endangered animals on the website, as well as discover what the IUCN does to address environmental issues all over the world.

Convention on International Trade in Endangered Species *(www.cites.org)*

CITES is an international agreement between governments that aims to ensure trade in wild animal species does not threaten their survival. It lists animals that are considered to be under threat from international trading, and makes laws accordingly.

US Fish and Wildlife Service *(www.fws.gov)*

This government organisation was set up to manage and preserve wildlife in the USA. It helps manage wildlife reserves, including those in wetland regions, and makes sure laws that protect endangered animals are properly enforced.

Do more...

Sign a petition

Petitions are documents asking governments or organisations to take action on something people are concerned about. Some of the organisations opposite have online petitions that you can sign to show your support for their campaigns.

Go to the zoo

Find out if your local zoo is involved in any captive-breeding programmes of wetland animals and go along to find out more. Just visiting the zoo helps support these programmes.

Adopt an animal

For a small contribution to some conservation organisations you get to 'adopt' a wetland animal. They will send you information about your adopted animal, and keep you up to date on all the conservation efforts in the area in which it lives.

Spread the word

Find out as much as you can about the threats to wetland animals and what people are doing to save them, then tell your friends and family. The more support conservation organisations have, the more they can do!

Read more...

Rivers and Wetlands
(Caring for the Planet)
by Neil Champion
(Franklin Watts, 2006)

Threatened Wetlands
(Protecting Our Planet)
by Catherine Chambers
(Wayland, 2009)

Usborne World of Animals
by Susannah Davidson and
Mike Unwin
(Usborne, 2007)

Wetlands (Biomes of the Earth)
by Peter D. Moore
(Facts on File, 2006)

Every effort has been made by the publisher to ensure that these websites contain no inappropriate or offensive material. However, because of the nature of the Internet, it is impossible to guarantee that the content of these sites will not be altered. We strongly advise that Internet access is supervised by a responsible adult.

Wetland Animals Quiz

Take this quiz to see how much you can remember about wetland animals. Look back through the book if you need to. The answers are on page 32.

1. Which type of wetland has trees growing in it?

2. Where will you find floodplains?

3. What is the soil in bogs called?

4. How do wetlands prevent flooding?

5. What is the name of the international treaty created to preserve wetlands?

6. Which is the largest wetland area in the world?

7. Which WWF programme is working to save Asian elephants?

8. In which countries are hippo populations increasing?

9. Which critically endangered crocodile may be saved by captive breeding?

10. How many Indian gharials are left in the wild?

11. Why are marsh deer under threat?

12. Where are sitatunga being studied to stop them becoming endangered?

13. What chemical is killing giant otters?

14. Which wetland types are home to coypus and capybaras?

15. Which introduced animal is killing the endangered water vole in the UK?

16. What is one of the greatest threats to the grey bat?

17. Which salamander breathes through gills?

18. Which swamp snake is the heaviest in the world?

19. What is the most endangered reptile in Australia?

20. What is threatening Australia's giant dragonflies?

Glossary

adapted changed in order to survive in new conditions.

amphibians animals that spend some of their time on land and some in water.

breeding mating and having babies.

captive breeding when endangered animals are specially bred in zoos or wildlife reserves so that they can then be released back into the wild.

census a count of the number of animals in a region.

civil war a war fought between groups of people within the same country.

climate change changes to natural weather patterns and temperatures caused by human activity.

conservation efforts to preserve habitats when they are under threat, have been damaged or destroyed.

crustaceans creatures with a skeleton outside their body and more than five pairs of legs.

degradation when the quality of the natural features of a habitat, such as its soil or water, grow worse.

drought a long period with a lower than average amount of rainfall in a particular region.

ecosystem all the different types of plants and animals that live in a particular area together with the non-living parts of the environment.

endangered at risk of becoming extinct.

estuaries coastal areas where rivers meet the sea.

extinct when an entire species of animal dies out, so that there are none left on Earth.

fens areas of marshy land created by water that lies on or close to the surface of the soil.

food chain a community of plants and animals in which each is eaten by another animal.

freshwater water that is not salty, such as the water in most rivers and lakes.

gills the parts of a fish's body that it uses to breathe.

habitat the place where an animal lives.

hydroelectric dams large structures used to control the flow of water from a river to generate electricity.

introduced species an animal that has been deliberately released into an area where it would not naturally occur.

irrigation watering crops by diverting water supplies with channels or ditches.

livestock animals kept by people for meat or milk.

logging cutting down trees.

mammals warm-blooded animals that usually give birth to live young.

mangroves areas of trees and shrubs, often with their roots in the water, which grow in tropical coastal regions.

mercury a poisonous liquid metal.

migration the movement of some animals from one place to another.

peat plant matter such as moss that has partly decayed.

pests animals that cause problems for people.

pollinating transferring pollen from one flower to another so that it can make seeds and grow into a new plant.

pollution man-made waste in the natural environment.

predators animals that hunt others for food.

protected status when animals are protected by law from hunting, trading or other human activities.

reptile a cold-blooded animal that lays eggs and usually has scales or plates on its skin.

reserves protected areas where the environment is carefully maintained for the benefit of wildlife.

saltwater water that contains salts, such as sea water.

sanctuary a special place where animals are protected or cared for if they are ill or injured.

species a type of animal or plant.

tusks the long 'teeth' on animals such as elephants.

vernal pools temporary pools of water.

Index

Numbers in **bold** indicate pictures

Quiz answers

1. Swamp; 2. Next to rivers; 3. Peat; 4. They take in water like a sponge; 5. Ramsar; 6. Pantanal; 7. Asian Rhino and Elephant Action Strategy; 8. Zambia, Chad and Ethiopia; 9. Philippine crocodile; 10. Less than 200; 11. Because of habitat loss and disease; 12. Lewa Wildlife Conservancy in Kenya; 13. Mercury; 14. Swamps, marshes, rivers and lakes; 15. American mink; 16. Disturbance in their caves; 17. Mudpuppy; 18. Green anaconda; 19. Western swamp tortoise; 20. Disturbance, habitat clearance and water pollution.

These are the lists of contents for each title in *Saving Wildlife:*

Desert Animals
What is a Desert? • Deserts Under Threat • Large Mammals • Sheep and Antelope • Outback Animals • Small Mammals • Desert Reptiles • Desert Amphibians • Amazing Insects • Spiders and Scorpions • Birds of Land and Air • In the Water • What Can We Do? • Desert Animals Quiz

Grassland Animals
Grassland Habitats • Grasslands Under Threat • Giants in the Grass • Cats of the Savannah • Wild Dogs • Hoofed Animals • Small Mammals • Curious Creatures • Reptiles • Minibeasts • Birds on the Ground • Birds in the Air • What Can We Do? • Grassland Animals Quiz

Mountain Animals
Mountain Habitats • Mountains Under Threat • Mountain Bears • Apes and Monkeys • Mountain Cats • Wild Dogs • Hoofed Animals • Small Mammals • Reptiles • Amphibians • Minibeasts • Birds • What Can We Do? • Mountain Animals Quiz

Ocean Wildlife
The Ocean Habitat • Oceans Under Threat • Whales • Dolphins and Porpoises • Other Marine Mammals • Marine Reptiles • Sharks • Commercial Fish • Tropical Fish • Shellfish • Sea Birds • Weird Wildlife • What Can We Do? • Grassland Animals Quiz

Polar Animals
Polar Habitats • Polar Regions Under Threat • Bears of the Cold Poles • Arctic Dogs • Hoofed Animals • Small Mammals • Aquatic Animals • Minibeasts • Penguin Paradise • Polar Birds • Whales in the Polar Waters • Fish and Other Sea Life • What Can We Do? • Polar Animals Quiz

Rainforest Animals
What is a Rainforest? • Rainforests Under Threat • Nature's Heavyweights • Big Cats • Forest Monkeys and Apes • Tree-Dwellers • Lizards Large and Small • Tropical Snakes • Amphibians • Minibeasts • In the Air • In the Water • What Can we Do? • Rainforest Animals Quiz

Wetland Animals
Wetland Habitats • Wetlands Under Threat • Large Mammals • Crocs in the Swamps • Wetland Deer • Semi-aquatic Creatures • Small Mammals • Amphibians • Reptiles • Wetland Birds • Minibeasts • Fish and Shellfish • What Can We Do? • Wetland Animals Quiz

Woodland and Forest Animals
Woodland and Forest Habitats • Forests Under Threat • Big Bears • Cats on the Prowl • Wild Dogs • On the Hoof • Medium Mammals • Small Mammals • By the Water • Slimy and Scaly Creatures • Minibeasts • Birds and Bats • What Can we Do? • Woodland and Forest Animals Quiz